THE BLUEPRINTS TO A
BLACK HEART

A Collection of Poems

Larry Foster

Copyright © 2017 Larry Foster

Printed in the United States of America

LIBRARY OF CONGRESS CATALOG # 2017964549

Contributing Writer: Kristina Mish
Cover Art by Erycka Cabrera
Cover design by Roel Sanchez

Published by Books by Anthony Parnell

DEDICATION

I dedicate this to the one that represents the past,
the future and the present. Whatever we leave behind and
whatever is yet to come, just know my words will heal.

PREFACE

Soul Literature

I'm not the one for words, at least not when it comes to writing lengthy essays or giving long speeches. Fortunately, over the last few years, poetry has become a tool, an outlet, and a voice for me to communicate what I think, what I feel and what I believe. This collection of poems, *The Blueprints to a Black Heart*, then, is a welcoming rendition to my past life experiences, my present mental and emotional state, and my future hopes and dreams.

The majority of my writing, since the beginning of my journey of discovering who I am as a poet, has been tailored to the genre of the "misunderstood." My poetry, I like to believe, is the voice of an illiterate soul. At the same time, it is through my own voice that I began to see the raw emotion behind my pain. This fed a greater desire to feel the depths of my pain's affection. Regretfully, for several years, my misguided mindset has led to many mistakes which have greatly hindered me from sustaining healthy relationships and mental stability.

As you read this book, hearing my thoughts and feeling my emotions, think not of the pain or misconstrued events that gave birth to them. Rather, think of the new outlook on life that gives them meaning. Move forward in reading this collection of poems with the understanding that perception does not have a one size fits all approach. In other words, remember that this written material was not created for just one concept to be perceived. It was written for the reader to grasp their own feelings while interpreting the context of my words.

Just as there are numerous ways to build a house, there are numerous ways to a black heart. I, therefore, encourage and challenge you to keep this mindset as you read through this book and as you progress in life through your own process of rehabilitation.

CONTENTS

FALSE HARVEST

The prophets word spread, a soul blind to its own truth

An existence justified by the natural instinct to migrate

Curious to see the world from an extraterrestrial point of view

Why conform for society?

How will I be able to seek out my own destiny
when I am shrouded by complacency?

If I put on a mask

I would have lived a lie

If I put on a mask

They will think I'm content

I'm tired of the questions

I'm tired of living by their expectations

If I put on that mask will everyone love me,
not realizing they drain me?

Everyone who has ever loved me has taken away from me

So, why should I have to conform to make others happy?

Why does my smile have such an effect on others' lives?

Why am I not allowed to have burdens of my own?

Am I only to carry the burdens of others - only to be left by them?

Only to be left with heavy shoulders?

The prophet said I would be blind to my own truth.

On second thought, I might just wear that mask

Maybe I should exceed their expectations

by becoming the blind truth that they see

THE BLUEPRINTS TO A BLACK HEART

Maybe I'm blind

Maybe I've deceived myself

Ignorant towards my own beliefs

Maybe I won't wear the mask Maybe I'll become the mask

THE DEVIL OF MY DEVIL

The Devil of My Devil
As thine lays me down to sleep
pray your soul to keep,
because if you die before I wake
your soul will surely be his to take.

Bear witness to a past tragedy
represented by a generation intolerable of mankind
due to incompetence and a lack of sympathy

Bear witness to this world's demise
The devil of the devil
was thine imaginary friend.
She smiled at him
as he grinned.

I've seen his hell
as he held me.
While I waited for morning to begin,
I saw his figure at my beds end

The devil of the devil was thine lust.
He covered her soul, she was my veil.

The devil of the devil was thine love.
A gift and a curse
from the hell above.

I was a wandering black hole
The day will come when I implode
That's when I will take in
the Omega and the Alpha.

How many depressions will I wake?
For every drip drop of knowledge
from horrid personal experiences.
Whose poor soul will be able to relate?

3

The devil of the devil, was thine home.
A dark place where there is no exit,
but from the entrance in which you came.

These loops of nightmares
repeated the torture of fate.
Victim to poetry, I shall not wake.
Dreams come true while reality manipulates

The devil of the devil
was thine reflection.
Are you so blind to him in the mirror?
Or are you blinded by the lack of affection?

The devil of the devil
was thine faith.
Lost in a garden he found his Eve,
the place where he birthed a religion,
for she knew his fruit was forbidden.

I was my own God
stranger only to myself.
Fighting with my own shadow
as I committed treason with each suicide

They will have a gala in my honor
when I damn all lost souls to eternity.
They are going to crown me Queen
and he, 'til death do us part, my King

The devil of the devil was thine thorn.
A dripping black heart with
roses dipped in blood.

The devil of the devil was thine guide.
As we walked through
the valley of the shadow of death,
I feared no evil.
For the devil of my devil, is thine.

Forgive me father for my sins.
Pray my soul to keep.
For when I wake,
my soul is surely his to take.

A SIREN'S APPEAL

I see no history past the present.
I hear no indulgences of care.
I feel no comfort in another's touch.
I taste only when bitten by lust.
I smell only death in a breath of fresh air.

I sensed her presence.
I answered the darkness.
She fulfilled my void.
She spoke truth to my reality.
Out of darkness was far from near.

I took heed from the darkness.
She said to drink when I became of thirst.
She said to eat when hunger arose.
She said to sleep when I grew weary.
She said to abandon all other desires.

Together we would see past the present history.
We would hear the screams of insanity.
We would feel nothing in pain's final form.
We would taste the deception of love.
We would smell the riches spoil.

I embraced the darkness.
She sheltered the misunderstood
as a sickened mind should and
as a tormented soul would.

In darkness's image,
I became whole.

GRAVITY

I had a dream
I was floating through space.
I was surrounded by wonders
that can never be described.
There was no sound.
My subconscious had nothing to say.

I felt nothing,
but everything.
I would see myself at times
like a camera switching angles.
I looked so small in space,
but I felt so grand.

Then I began to fall
and my dream
now became a nightmare.
I could hear screams inside my head.
My body became numb.
All I could do was witness as fate took its course.

I saw myself speeding rapidly towards a planet
as if something was calling me home.
As my body entered the atmosphere
I began to contemplate.
Where was I headed?

I was content beyond imagination
Why was I needed here?
What I saw on the surface
was a wonder that could never be described.

Like a star gazing upon the sky
as your gravity pulled me to its core.
Your smile became clear
as I drew near.
Our bond forevermore.

I GREW OLD

I used to imagine us
well you and I that is.
Lost somewhere happy on this earth.
Lost in each other's will to carry on.

My visions where so vivid of us.
The things we would do,
the places we would go,
the love that we would create to last a lifetime and another.
It was all so clear

But,

A visitation of home altered my imagination.
I saw you and I saw her and then him
Same eyes looking at me seeing everything while I saw nothing.
I felt nothing
And wanted nothing,
but to have never existed in their lives

Now the reality that I see is me indulged in my
own will power to carry on.
Focused on the things I was meant to do,
the places I was meant to go,
And the love...
the love that I was meant to live without.

Now I find myself —
Everything in my past irrelevant
Every thought relevant to my future —
Reaching mental heights once suppressed by the thought of love.
My emotions,
well the lack thereof.

We were never meant to be
only dreams for a dreamer.
I'll never know who you and I were
that is the unrelenting question

INDIFFERENT

You made me smile when I knew I shouldn't.
You gave me warmth when I knew I couldn't.
You took me when I didn't want to be taken.

You could say you chose me.
You should see your eyes when you're with me.
So full of passion and regret.
You always were scared, but unmoved.

Our first kiss, I caught you by surprise.
The second one you took me by surprise.
A feeling that could never be understood by the world.
We started something, not knowing that it would end.

I was scared, I made up excuses
I denied you, but you knew…
You knew you had me.
That I would be yours forever.

You broke me,
took me apart,
and put me back together.
You planned this from the start.

I believed your intentions.
You said it was just us.
That no one could ever understand
and that your love was my destiny.

I fell for you.
I gave everything up for you.
I needed you.
I still need you.

But you're gone.
In your house,
you left me standing there all alone and
you left me without a place to go.

You left me with words,
but no ears to listen.

Now I can't go a day without agony.
Now I can't trust those who express their care.
Now I don't believe in my worth.
I look back and it hurts.
How could you leave something you discovered?

MEMORIES OF US:
A GIFT AND A CURSE

Our hands like magnets bonded to love.
Our eyes would say all the words we didn't know how to.
We became a gift and a curse,
a bond where we became one and no longer two.

The way your body felt when you pulled me closer.
Making sense of the world,
your lips would take away the pain.

Every day I long for you.
Just a moment with you.
Every day I yearn for it.

Our souls bound to forever.
An internal bond that reaches out for each other,
as if our souls were connected.

I feel your touch hundreds of miles away.
I feel it as it makes me stutter inside.
I close my eyes and there you are
smiling, reaching out for my love.

Why does life hold you hostage?
Why won't it give you back to me?
Life's a disease without you.

But hope gives me strength.
It gives me strength to carry on.
Knowing that tomorrow is a step closer
to a dream that one day will be my reality.

CLOSE ENOUGH

I never feel like you're close enough
Even when you're close I feel like you're not close enough
I'm so in love with you, I forget about reality
I forget that our morality reflects our consequences
That our consequences are a direct reflection of which we are
Every time I reflect I only see my mistakes
All the mistakes that has led me to this point
What am I trying to prove?
A point.
I never feel like you're close enough
Come Close,
Enough

TUG OF WAR

There's a big war going on in my soul
and I know nobody feels it but you.
I know you're on my side,
feet planted side by side.

Life forever tugging
pulling us away,
but our feet are rooted,
hands scarred from pain.

There's a big war going on in my soul
and I know nobody feels it but you.
I know you're on my side,
feet planted side by side.

I look across the line,
so many contenders.
some familiar, some yet to come.
For our battle has just begun.

There's a big war going on in my soul
and I know nobody feels it but you.
I know you're on my side,
feet planted side by side.

Sometimes I even see myself
as I look across the line.
Sickens me seeing the scars I've left
so many on your shaking hands.

There's a big war going on in my soul
and I know nobody feels it but you.
I know you're on my side,
feet planted side by side.

But you still stand by my side.
You've been rooted since day one.
Against all odds, you stood alone.

Larry Foster

There's a big war going on inside your soul.
Just know I feel it too.

Know I'm on your side,
feet planted side by side.
Rest my love; put your faith in me.
Now it's my time
to take the lead.

There's a big war going on inside your soul,
just know I feel it too.
Know I'm on your side,
feet planted side by side.

My hands are bigger
so, let's see life come at me.
You couldn't break my Queen,
So what are you going to do
in the presence of her King.

There's a big war going on inside your soul,
just know I feel it too.
Know I'm own your side,
feet planted side by side.

There will be no peace,
we can't afford to lose.
Our only option is glory and
our only hope is time.

There's a big war going on inside our souls,
our feet planted side by side.
I'd rather die, than to see
life pulls us across that line.

So, from this day forward
for better, for worse
for richer and for poorer.
In sickness and in health
until death do us part,
we will fight this war together
our feet planted side by side
all to hear God say...
Do you take this woman to be your bride?

13

FACE TO FACE

She wondered how she would feel
as she slipped into her pretty little heels.
Is this how the tall girls felt?
Oh, the short end of this stick she was dealt.

He wondered how he would feel
as he dressed in layers.
Is this how the buff guys felt?
Oh, the scrawny end of the stick he was dealt.

She wondered how she would feel
as she relaxed her hair.
Is this how the straight-haired girls felt?
Oh, the nappy end of the stick she was dealt.

He wondered how he would feel
as he started up the hill.
Is this how all the skinny people felt?
Oh, the chubby end of the stick he was dealt.

She wondered how she would feel
as she applied makeup to her face.
Is this how the pretty girls felt?
Oh, the imperfect end of the stick she was dealt.

A mirror on the wall.
A reflection of a desire.
A picture in painting.
The only reflection we require.

Why do we aim to mirror ourselves of things we lack?
All the while miscalculating our perfections
shadowed by society's obsession with your reflection.

An internal lack of esteem
creating a demand for alteration.
A beauty so natural and priceless
watch stigmatisms sway a nation.

14

DOMESTICATED

Hit me once shame on you.
Hit me twice shame on me.
But when the shame puts the blame
on a society that refuses to call it by its name
we create: (or, possibly, "we have: ..."):

A fatherless son subjugated to an enraged father.
An overbearing mother subjugated to an abusive husband.
A child in the care of foster subjugated to an adopted love.
A dog subjugated to an aggressive owner.

These people all have a commonality.
They are taught to sit in the presence of their master.
Scolded at any signs of self-dependence.
Dependent for food and other essential commodities.

Treated as we would a dog
these relatives of abuse have become domesticated.
Hindered from happiness at the thought of
abandoning their aggressor.
Be their voice by numbing their pain.
Numb their pain by learning their name.

RA

If all around me is your gravity
then I will always gravitate towards you.
A constant rotation of uncertainty.
I get lost in my lack of essence
as I transition from black to white and back
to that gray area again.
Nothing seems constant,
but my will to gravitate towards you.

Am I the center of your universe?
Or just an epicenter in your solar system?
Give me life, show me the truth
all the while I gravitate towards you.
So illuminating yet so far away.
The closer I get to you, the closer I get to the truth.

Is it true that to stand by your side means to be
the author of my demise?
Why must you sustain life yet keep us at bay?
I feel lost in your gravity.
Why am I just a past time of your history?

Every morning I wake to you illuminating the way.
I wonder your destiny, I wonder about your uncertainty.
But one thing I cannot deny
and that no matter the de ja vu,
I will always gravitate towards you.

DREAMS AND NIGHTMARES

My dreams kept me awake.
My nightmares sheltered my fate.
I was lost in the winter when I came to you.
A lost soul who was addicted to an endless de ja vu.

The place where I laid my head
wasn't where I rested my soul.
A ride or die approach
to show how you played your role.

With me all alone
and you with no offspring to call your own.
The way you sheltered my soul
through your motherly love and affection.
I found a new truth.

Memories on replay,
a true gift and a true curse.
I was lost in the nightmare of reality.
You became my Atlas,
the foundation to my sanity.

The way you looked at me
and the way I looked back at you.
Oftentimes I ponder and daydream.....
During that winter, where I would be without you?
You reached out to me like an olive branch saving grace.
We created a bond that would transcend fate.
You had your own personal droughts.
Yet your shoulder stayed on call, readily waiting.

Even on your worst day
you would set aside a part of you.
You always found a way
to nurture me through.
My admiration for your resolve
over time became the basis of my strength.

My dreams still keep me awake.
My nightmares still shelter my fate.
One truth became clear, through thick and thin
to the naked eye......
In my dreams and in my nightmares,
you are my one true ride or die.

Larry Foster

SOLD AS IS

If beauty is only skin deep.
Imagine the worth of a human defined by their quality of their insides.
Imagine an industry based on the demand of lust.
The consumption of goods
a priceless human commodity.

Millions of innocent women
birthed to be the essence of another.
Violated beyond reasoning by savage beasts.
Bought with no intent to ever be worth more than a past time.
Abused, entered...the daily renditions of these souls.

Such flaws in our society.
The ability for a gender controlled civilization
to introduce its counterpart
to a life of submissiveness.
Where is the voice for these slaves?
What is the response for their transgressions?

The inhumane thought of currency manipulating their destiny.
Experiences that can only be dreamt in the form of nightmares.
An inability to fathom the worth of their life.
One must wonder,
how many unauthorized personnel does it takes before they break.

PAPER PLANE

There's a lot that goes
into making a paper plane.

You need the paper to create.
You need the experience to manipulate.
Paper coming from the trees that give us life.
Experience from life that gives us the ability to create.

Trees are the one thing that gives life.
But a tree must die
for this paper plane to fly.

Someone had to harvest the tree.
Another had to cultivate the tree.
Someone had to jack the lumber.
Someone processed the tree into paper.

Then comes your attempt to fold that paper.
Sometimes even failing over and over.
But you will fold and fold again.
You'll fold until you're able to make that plane fly.

A plane needs wings to fly.
They both need to be exactly alike.
To be exact, for or a plane to fly
a plane needs two wings to fly.

I guess what I'm trying to say….
Is there's a lot that goes into making a paper plane.
Thank you for being my other wing.
I thank life for being our body.
And thank life for teaching us how to fly.

TRILOGY

I love you
I'll prove to you these three words.
For if you asked me for a garden
I would plant two.
For if you asked of me a home
I would build for you.
For if you asked for my soul
I would happily give that too.
For ilf you asked of me my last words
and if death was upon me.
With three words left to breathe
I would utter those three,
Rest in peace

OUR OVERTURE

To ignore our love means to hinder
our "To be" or "Not to be."
The look in your eyes says I hate deception.
All the while you wait for love.
A burden begins to take its toll.

It's not until she held him close
that every moment she missed began to show.
It's not until he held her close
that every moment he missed began to show.

It's in the way you move.
The way you dance around me like I am your sun.
It's the way you reach for my hand.
The way our overture has just begun.

What I felt from you
was a kiss that could comfort a soul,
was a connection that was overdue,
it was a desire to be made whole.

A family one day to confide.
Have faith in every word I wrote.
An appeal for you to stand by my side.
Just know this is our first love note.

A man has vision, but hardly sees
that the eyes in front of him
are the eyes that will one day bring him to his knees.

A note to my future bride
I just hope one day you'll see,
that I will let nothing hinder
our "To be" or "Not to be."

AMPHIBIOUS REFLECTION

Staring back at you
I forget that we exist independently of one another.

Staring back at you
I'm mesmerized at the loneliness of codependency.

Staring back at you
I see societies overlapping existence between here and there.

Staring back at you
I'm amazed at your ability to thrive in any environment.

Staring back at you
I acknowledge your complexity and the simplicity of your intellect.

Staring back at you
I'm taken back by your ability to manipulate our de ja vu.

CHECK MATE

Could you spare a little change?
Just a little change of heart.
You see, when you met me
I already knew who you were from the start.

But I ignored you.
You know how kids like to play.
But, I saw you first.
Bad intentions and all.

I let you come over,
even let you come close.
As you poured and poured
reveling your innermost.

I just stared at you
because destiny saw us first.
I destroyed all your hopes and dreams
even though I wanted the same.
And here you are still.
Isn't that the definition of insane?

You thought it was over,
but I caught you by surprise.
Ha, you thought it was over,
My kiss the alpha to your demise.
You almost crashed the whip,
As we spoke lip to lip.

Look at us now four years' in,
still got you coming over.
But now I'm in your corner.
Maybe you saw me first,
doubtful,
but you've gotten good at playing the game.

But never forget
I saw you first
and the game isn't over.
In hindsight, the board was flipped.

I'll always be your first
and you'll always be my last.
But you should ask yourself,
what's a pawn to a king
if the pawn always goes first?

ARCHITECT OF MY DESIGN

My life is yours and yours mine,
this is the bond soulmates share.
Whether this was paradox or by design,
time will act as our jury
and fate our one true judge.

If all this was built by design
our truth has acted as the blueprints,
our strength has been the foundation,
and our story was the process.

Each page has already been written.
With each chapter serving its purpose.
If we could read the story backwards,
we would only find ourselves where we started.

The world in which we were conceived
in a way has always been cursed by opposites.
The constant struggle between opposites
has defined humanity, and thus defined us.

Whether it's the balance of good and evil.
Do we believe the truth or begin to believe our lie?
Do we stay where we are or go where we belong?
Did we find love or was it just the veil of lust?

Opposites attract the most uncommon of our kind,
all the while opposing the fundamental beliefs we all share.
By design and through free will
we have been cursed to contemplate our past and our future.

I believe this was all built by design.
A design created by the heavens to be dammed by hell.
Opposites never meant to attract.
Maybe therefore our crossroad
will always be the time spent between life and death.

ASYLUM SEEKER

Our names are a soul that was never whole.
Two soulful judges that will never pass judgment against its soul.
As we seek out other souls to be made whole,
Only the two souls who were meant to be whole
Will be enough to make two halves a whole.
All the other souls will only be enough
to make their soul miss it's whole.
Even if it that half makes it whole,
two halves of a whole
will eventually become one soul.
I hope you realize my soul only shares a beat to your soul,
because my soul carries on even without being whole.

FINDING NEVER

You'll always be my first.
You'll always be my last.
The first to show me love.
The last to steal my soul.

I'm happiest when I'm with you.
Time never seeming to exist.
Even with knowing our destiny,
we would always take the risk.

The risk of feeling loved
even for a moment in history.
As you held me in your arms
my soul would feel at home.

The way we kissed,
feeding my soul.
The way we held hands
no longer the feeling of alone.

I loved the way you walked.
The confidence around your air.
I loved the way you smelled.
Your skin so comforting.
I loved the way you smiled.
The little things we did to see each other laugh.

I miss our night rides
As we found new places to create memories.
I miss our talks
as cocky as they were.
I miss hearing your voice
as you whispered in my ear.
I miss when you pulled me closer
when you couldn't stand it any longer.

Now you're gone
after so many years.
Knowing that I can never see you again
I contemplated tears.

I feel numb.
Numb from being apart
from having to carry on.

Each day
I wonder what life would be
if there was such a place for you and me.
I wonder where life would take us
if I had my way.
I wonder why life would show me you
but make it impossible for everyone else to see.

As I lay here
wishing you were by my side.
Wishing you were here
to take away my agony.

I'm afraid that you'll never return.
And that I'll spend the rest of my life
trying to find my way back home.
Only to stumble every day on the pathway of uncertainty.

I only hope that if I never find my way through.
If you should ever pass before I do.
When my time comes,
I hope my soul finds its way back to you.

PLAY ON REPEAT

Eyes closed, sex became our melody.
As I laid in your arms
we danced in the sheets.
Just close enough to hear
each other's beat.

Our bodies intertwined.
Why we ever left this place.
The place we were at peace.

Away from them,
Away from hate,
Away from pain,
Away from society.

Your kisses long... passionate.
Each time making me want for more.
Grooving to our own melody.
Inside of each other we danced,
while we would hold hands.

I miss being in your arms.
I miss being at peace.
I'm missing the best part of me.
Put our melody on repeat
and forever in our insanity.

CARETAKER

I watch you watch him.
I listen to your conversations.

The therapist to my aroma therapy.

Your eyes tell the truth.
How you perceive him.

He wonders your story.
What makes you who you are today?

He pays attention to you shake, more than your words.
He wants to cry, but he's tired from crying.

I'm tired of being weak.
I want to go, but he wants to stay.

We argue whether you can help.
All the while maintaining conversation with you.

Bi-polar with a mix of insanity.
Spilt personalities inside a blank canvas.

You have a complex mind before you.
Save him before he saves himself.

Before we are no more.

TREASON FROM WITHIN

When I reached this point,
death was the only option.
Death was the only decision.
I had decided to kill myself.

But when I woke,
I felt empty inside.
I felt dead, but I was alive.
Had I committed suicide against my being?

I didn't even recognize the person in the mirror.
He looked ready, strong, unmoved by emotions or society.
He looked detached.
He smiled and I smiled back.
Had I in fact killed myself and let something else take control?

I smiled at myself.
As thoughts ran through my head.
I saw myself detached, but wired.
I saw myself alone, but inspired.
I saw myself quit, but ambitious.

Memories, they were gone.
Bonds, they were severed.

I hope that this is the lowest point in my life.
I had killed myself to save myself.
I had committed treason to save myself.

STARE

What if the real me isn't the me that I want to be?
What if I don't recognize myself?
How will I live behind a mask?
One that looks like me,
but isn't me.

I've been with so many
I can't figure out who I was real with.
I can't figure out when I was being me.
I can't figure out when it was real.

Was it you that showed me how to fly?
Or was it you that showed me passion?
Or was it you that made...
that made me believe in eternity?

I can't figure out when I was me.
Now I'm stuck here trying to find myself.
So many missing pieces.
Scared to put myself back together.
Scared of what I wouldn't find.

How will I love if I don't love myself?
How will I trust if I don't trust myself?
How will I believe in something I can't see?
When I don't believe in what I see in front of me.

Hopefully standing in front of this mirror
I will find who I am.
I'll even figure out who I was real with
and maybe that person that I find
will be holding the mask of my reflection.

LOOP

I can tell you some things.
Tell you some things
to make you fall to your knees.
Make you beg please.
But luckily, I don't need your sympathy.

What I've become isn't what you've come to need.
What I want is what most would not dare.
What I need is for you to get on your knees and beg for eternity.
Lay on your back and fulfill my fantasy.

Who I am is who I've become.
Become something more than those who've failed to overcome.
Now you see that my presence
shall exceed my reputation.
My goals will be accomplished beyond expectation.

Whether the future shall hold a life surrounded by plenty,
or a life surrounded by none.
My destiny has already been lived.
I'll always have the audacity to carry on.

CLOSER

If you saw me there
If you saw me dancing all alone
Dancing all alone to our song
Would you leave me to dance alone?

If you saw me walking in the street
Dancing to our favorite beat
Like the times when we were high
Would you keep on walking by?

If you saw me on my last feet
Wandering through life
Lost in the transition of hope
Would you throw me your rope?

If you saw me at my best
What you've always wanted
A picket fence around me
Would that make you come home?

If I saw you there
dancing all alone to our favorite beat,
I wouldn't leave you all alone.
I would dance with you all night long.

If I saw you walking in the street
Grooving to our favorite beat
If I saw you at your best
The person I knew you could be

I would return home
to never again leave you alone.
Life showed me you.
I haven't given up on life, so I won't give up on you.

SHORT-TERM MEMORY

The day we met,
maybe it was fate that brought us together,
time that broke us apart,
and our destiny to never be.

Maybe we weren't meant to last a lifetime
or live destined to be entwined.
Two lovers caught in an endless rhyme.

But where does that leave the memories?
Where does that leave the love?
Where does that leave the pain?
Where does that leave the promises?

A journey planned for two,
that was the plan for me and you.
Though you may have strayed.
Though our love begins to fade.

Have faith in me,
have faith in destiny,
have faith that over time
that fate never changes its mind.

A LIFETIME GLANCE

Your love, what I've fought for blindly
ever since your eyes told me to.
If I could just stare into your eyes
watching you smile for the rest of my life.
That's all I would need to do.

I close my eyes and there you are
smiling, reaching out for my love.
Is this just a dream?
Or is this my reality?

Countless nights I've dreamt of you
then I wake up from a dream.
A dream that's left me alone.
How can feelings be so deep?
That I feel you when I sleep.

Through all the smiles,
the lies, the tears and the pain.
Through it all our souls...
the only thing that seems to remain the same.

How I long for the love.
Longing for the love that took away the pain.
Our souls intertwined
meant to last a lifetime.

And if I could spend eternity with you in a stairwell
I would, because that's where I fell.
Where I fell in love with you.
I'm sick without you, but your love gives me strength.
Your love gives me strength to carry on
knowing that tomorrow is a step closer
to a dream that one day will be my reality.

And if there is ever any doubt,
any doubt in your mind about these two lovers stuck
in an endless rhyme,
just realize you were meant to be mine.

AN EMOTIONLESS RANT

As I sit at the edge of the sea,
I look out.
I am calm, relaxed, and free.

Music without the influence of words flowing through my head,
I've been in this place before.
I remember the state of doubt that shadowed me.

Now my perception is as clear as life itself.
My ambitions, my dreams
are floating around me.

I have much more to accomplish before they can be met.
I have many improvements to be made on myself.

In time my body will heal.
My mental state will reveal
my true love's everlasting will.

I find it selfish to give it to one person.
Downright dangerous to entrust it to anyone.

Yes, I've learned this from my past
at the cost of my solitude,
I can accomplish so many things and affect so many lives.

THIS VERY MOMENT

I'm sorry for ever hurting you.
Since that day I've been lost without you.
I promise to never hurt you again.
I'd rather die than to lose my best friend.

I just want to get back to you
for things to be the same.
How I long for the love.
Longing for the love that took away the pain.

So many before you have left scars on my soul.
Over the years the scars have taken its toll.

But you're the only one who's ever touched my soul.
Our souls intertwined
meant to last a lifetime.

Everything that we've been through.
It's this very moment
what I've fought for blindly.
Ever since your eyes told me to.

I promise to love you.
I promise to always be here.
I promise to protect you.
I promise to please you.

I stand here before you,
waiting for you to take my hand.
Hoping that you'll say yes,
and come home to your man.

STUCK IN AN ENDLESS RHYME

If I ever let you go,
you should know
to set you free
would be
to lose a part of me.

I love you,
but things were never meant to be the same.
Missing you is always on my brain.
Times have changed.
Maybe two, maybe three,
maybe one day we could be.

Just you and I,
two souls caught in time.
Stuck in an endless rhyme.

Say you will,
you'll never leave,
never let go
of what we have.

Because what we have
means the world to me.
Words cannot explain
how I feel, how I've changed.

All I need is your love,
beauty next to none.
You're heaven's gift from above.

If I ever let you go,
you should know

that I would live in agony
knowing that
I let our love die.

You're the sunshine
that lights up my sky.
All we have is time
but only life knows the answer
to this endless rhyme.

DESIRE

I've never experienced real love,
only the love that strays.
Only love that takes and doesn't give.
Love that asks, but doesn't share.

I relinquish that love,
for that is selfish love.
I aspire the truth in love.
The love that you give me.

Love that can make a man stronger.
Love that is unselfish and unwavering.
Love that heals the soul.
Love that supports through transgression and progression.
Love that provides comfort.
Love that is secure and the basis of growth.
Love that is constant.
Love that sacrifices and makes due.
Love that pleases.

I embrace true love.
True love that can lead to something far greater than happiness.
I want this love.

GROWING PAINS

I live in hell
A mentally unstable hell
My thoughts shroud my judgement
Pain has taken form in personality

Birth and death
Life is to be viewed as a blessing
Both lost and given each day
Life is the only constant thing in our lives

How can someone view life as a gift?
When they have been gifted pain that is chronic
Only to be described as a curse

Even now as I begin to type I can feel the pain pass through my body
A constant pinching, like a relentless bee sting
Inflammation caused by a burning sensation

The agony of this pain is unwavering
How does one find joy, when they aren't
comfortable in their own body?
How does one find happiness, when they are greeted
by pain every waking morning?

I believe that death is the cure
My mind has made living a disease
Contemplating suicide each day
Trying to convince myself that the pain of my loved
ones isn't worth my freedom

I feel weak, slowly withering both physically and mentally
I feel obstructed, unable to sympathize
I can't remember life before pain
I can only hope for a life without it

44

What I would give for a day
Just one day in this hell
To wake up and be gifted the opportunity of
letting my day decide my mood
Instead of waking each day considering sleep,
only to look forward to the pain

TREE OF LIFE

The greatest experiences in life
is watching you burn.
Watching you sparkle.
Filling the air with passion and love.
Slowly becoming my drug.

As you begin to vibe
I begin to rhyme.
Thinking back to
when all we had was time.

I get a little higher.
Now it's just you and I.
Pains get a little lighter.
Now it's just you and I.

Forever you and I will vibe.
Air becomes filled of passion and love.
Forgetful of hurt and envy.
Free of that which is selfish.
Fond of what just is.

Now it's you and I standing here.
Where did they all go?
Promises of forever
end all too soon.

A tree setting fire
to a past as dark as the ashes that it left.
But in this ash spawns hope,
that whatever yesterday left behind,
and today may bring,
tomorrow will heal.

With each burning desire.
A psychedelic approach to my reality.
The gateway drug to the truth.
Give me life as I burn away my agony

CIVIL WAR

I think we found eternity.
I think we found insanity.
I think we found love.
I think we found hate.

When I first saw you
I knew....
I knew that day would be the first
of many days of finding forever.

I hid myself from you.
Not wanting to be hurt again.
Not realizing all the while
I was hurting you.

You make me want to get as far as I possibly can.
Knowing I'll spend everyday away from you
thinking about you.
It's a vicious cycle, I know.

I think we found fate.
I think we were meant.
I think we found forever.
I think we found only good for now.

Why do we continue to play?
Is it our love that makes us return?
Or to see who can win this time around?

I should have hope this time around
that you would keep things real.
Ha, the crazy thing is even when you're fake I forgive you.
Even when I stumble
you always seem to be my spine.

I wonder what the word is for people like us.
Toxic, unhealthy, deadly, crazy, incompatible?
Those aren't words for people in love,
those are words for those who are at war.

Each day this battle carries on,
neither side will ever win or lose.
So instead of proving them right,
I'll offer you an olive branch made for two
just to show I love you.

EVERY TIME

I stopped counting.
I stopped counting your goodbyes
and started calculating your hellos.

What keeps you coming back?
Is it the cum back?
What keeps you interested?
Or is the fact that I can come and go as I please.
The fact that I can put you on your knees
or is it that you love them,
but worship eternity.

What has our lust become.
Feels like a rush.
I want to go right, but I keep left.
Feels like a never-ending circle.

Always coming back to start
where we began.
Where we always seem to end.
Baby,
I swear you got that thing.

This game we play.
One on one.
But always playing on the same team.
Feelings so deep...
A dream within a dream.

It's crazy to think that the one that causes the pain,
the same source of peace,
the soul that drives you insane,
they are all one in the same.

I get lost in your lies
the same way I get lost in your eyes.
Maybe it's just my imagination.
Maybe you're just a figment of my imagination.

How can that be?
I feel so alive when you're with me.
I feel so irrelevant when you leave.
I always end up on my knees.

I stopped counting your goodbyes
and started calculating your hellos.
You're my everything.
You're all I need.

All I need
is for you to
Know my desires and become my ambition.
Remember my fears.
Inspire me to want more.
Show me eternity and become my serenity.

Tame my soul.
Invite me to bed.
Numb my pain and become my prescription.
Atone for our sins.

See... I stopped counting your goodbyes.
I calculated your hellos.
This time will we be different.
Than every time.

EVERMORE

A lifetime of passion
An eternity of pain
Never to be forgotten
Each day a day closer to the next

Infidelity, the root of our pain
Two sides to every story
The lies tear us apart
Our truth brings us closer

As definite as any tattoo
Greater than any sexual desire
More stimulating than any dope
Than any instinctive emotion
As sure as any faith

Our love accepts one another
For not how we see the other
But for whom we are

Your voice calms me
My silence bothers you
Our presence comforts

Belonging to one another
Our souls blind to a time
Where we exist independently
Our bond forevermore

ENDLESS CIRCLE

An ending to a beginning that was never meant to end.
No more hope just confined to memories of the past.
Maybe it's premature to call the game,
but then again, it's been six consecutive seasons.
I write this with no hope.
The more I type,
the more I reflect on your actions.
Words become less important.
Part of me just wants to walk to you, hoping you'd see me.
Maybe that would change your mind.
It feels like you're scared to be around me.
Because it would change your mind.

Or maybe I'm the one who's scared.
Hopefully, someone makes up their mind.
Every day I say no more.
I tell myself to ignore.
But how do I walk away from
a beginning that was never meant to end.

POWERLESS

They say....
Why does everything that's supposed to be bad make you so good?
I say....
Why not take the good with the bad if it gets you
through to another day?

An addiction that makes you feel.
An addiction that gets you through.
An addiction that allows you to be you.

To say I need you would be true.
Not because I want you,
but because you embody forever.

Like a child in the womb
you give me warmth where I need it most.
Like a hug from the inside
you give me warmth where I need it most.

I remember our first day.
I was sitting down.
I remember it like it was yesterday.
I threw my head back
and you started to take over.

Ever since then we've been inseparable.
Do you remember that night?
So many nights you were there.

Through the good and the bad.
You've seen me on my knees.
You've seen me at my lowest.
You were my atlas
when I couldn't stand on my own.

You were my rhythm
when I needed to dance.
When I need to let go
you began to flow.

An addiction that takes you higher.
To feel your warmth as I come alive.
I'll never stop throwing my head back.
I'm powerless towards the desire.

TIME ZONES

I'd wake up only to find out you were on your way to sleep.
But for me my day had just begun.
It wasn't enough for me to spend my days awake,
while you lay in slumber.
It wasn't enough for you to be asleep,
knowing I wouldn't be awake to join you throughout your day.

So, worlds apart we switched our schedules.
I would take my naps in broad daylight
while you slept in the dark.
The light from your computer would blind your eyes
while on my side the sun lit up the skies.

We were worlds apart it would seem.
My days, your nights.
My rise, your fall.
My mornings, your evenings.

From the start, we were opposites.
Always living separate lives.
But we sacrificed our times to be apart of each other's present.
I remember the nights you would stay up late
just to say good morning.
I remember the kisses blown as you saw me off to sleep.
Sometimes I ask myself how those two kids survived
living in different times.

We became figments of our imagination.
Lost in thoughts of being together.
We became lovers unbound to time.
In our hearts, we stood still.
All the while the world around us in constant rotation.

When I look back on how we went against time
I ponder on how we could be in each other's present.
Without looking at our past
in remembrance of the future we once had.

Time zones apart we created daylight savings.
One soul willing to jump forward.
The other willing to fall back.
Now it only seems that we leap away from each other.

Maybe time will repeat itself.
Hopefully one day each zone will end where we began.
Two lovers and friends caught in time.
Hopefully one day its travelers will settle down again.

CONTEMPLATION

Things end, but memories last forever,
I wonder if the memories are enough
to bring us back together.

From time to time I reminisce.
Usually drinking that or smoking this.
How we used to play with each other.
So, puerile and lost
to the agony that was meant to be.

In a world like this
where family is quick to judge
and a society not ready to budge.
I often felt handicapped.
Me versus you versus the world point of view.

As I walked down the road on a path familiar to us,
I found myself walking alone.
Sporadic memories of our past
in hindsight, we were never going to last.

But an urge came over my soul
for closure.
I began to dial your number.
I began to lose my composure.

What I need is not an end.
Things end but memories last forever,
but then again,
I ponder if memories are enough to bring us back together.

HANGERS

One day I want a walk-in-closet
big enough for me and you.
So, we can read these words
and hopefully walk out together.
These words were all for you.
He who will not be named.
He for who I still feel the same.

The same as when I first saw you.
Full of life, the way you looked at me.
I didn't know you then.
I don't know you now.
I wonder if he knew.
I wonder if he would care.
So many words written about him
I know he would care.

You see he's the type...
He's the type that would...
He's the type to claim solitary,
but the type to then enjoy missionary.
That's just who he is.
He's attractive to say the least
with the build that of a beast.
A smile that would drive you crazy
and skin fit for Ms. Daisy.

Man, he's inspired so much pain.
If he ever found out
about all these words...
I could see him now
piercing down.

I could see him shaking his head
picking up his phone,
making me read along.

It was all supposed to be a secret.
A secret from whom?
I wonder if he hid it from himself.
What he will fail to see
these words weren't written for him,
they were written for me.

All from your love
and from pain caused by secrecy,
I found a way to find peace and harmony.
You see I wrote it all down
hoping you would read every poem.
Hoping that you would feel ashamed
for starting, but never finishing,
for leaving a soul without a home
for coming back only to never unpack,
for making me feel as though I was only worth an hour,
for those nights I would cry alone in the shower.

I hope these words make you see
in my world, you were a part of me.
I hope these words make you see
without you, serenity could never be me.
I know your intentions were there.
I know you loved me your own way.
That I'm special in your lonely world.
That you did your best to comfort me.
It was always you who came to me.

But what you did in the end.
What you did was pick them over me.
You chose to stay hidden.
You chose society and your family.
Over the one you called your destiny.

You broke your promise.
You forgot your words.
You said it was just us two,
that each other would do
and that nobody would understand.
Remember, I was the crack house
and you the crackhead.
I wonder when you got clean,
because you forgot to clean out the hangers in your closet.

THE BLUEPRINT

When it's pushed instead of pulled,
the force of gravity
creates a universe that is imperfect.
It manifests a reality that can never be accepted.
Dreams only fulfilled for the unconscious.

Pushing you away
is always what I excelled at.
It was my way of showing you the love I could never give you.
The love you deserved.

Unknowingly I created a void in myself.
One that I can't fill, nor have the desire.
I birthed a monster.
One full of pain and darkness.

My soul has become imperfect,
detached from reality.
Unwilling to accept its fate.
Rarely ever willing to succumb to your will.

Now I live a dream deferred by reality.
One where you and I are one.
Now I live a life of regret.
Faced to witness the birth every morning,
tattooed across my chest of the one who saved me from myself.
Whose love sheltered me from darkness.
Now I'm displaced.
Where there was protection,
darkness covers my shadow.
Where there was love,
vindictive thoughts take the place of emotions.
Where there was hope,
angst shuns the audacity.

A dark heart dripping
as thorns pierce through it.
Roman Numerals of the Alpha and the Omega carved into its roses.
The portrait finally one with its canvas.
The blueprint finally accomplished.

TIME TRAVELERS

Do you believe two souls could withstand the test of time?
You once asked could all our problems be solved
if we pushed rewind.
Two souls intertwined.....
Do you believe that there's an end to this endless rhyme?

Sometimes I get the feeling that we have been here before.
The feeling that our souls have been at odds through the ages.
Why can't I remember our first hello?
Could it be that we've slipped through time?
It appears we were running from each other,
but we always found ourselves running in the
same direction for cover.

We always seem to meet others along the way,
but never anyone strong enough to keep our souls at bay.
A game of cat and mouse.
Oh, a game we love to play.

I've been known to take things too far.
More than ever in this lifetime
I've pushed you to your limits.
I just hope, my actions aren't enough for you to say goodbye.

You see, I've been without you before.
Many times, through our travels, so many days I've spent alone.
Subconsciously pushing you away
in hopes that you would start a life,
one where our souls are at bay.

Through our travels
we've experienced heaven.
Through our travels
we've weathered hell.
Writing this now miles apart
I realize I miss being whole.

CRAVE

An addict discovers while a doctor heals.
Family members cry while a dealer reaps.
The halfway home is always full.
The mental ward meant for the misunderstood.
The distinction between addicting and invigorating.
What dictates an addiction's ability to become toxic?
How does one begin healing
before they can accept they are sick?
How does one become vindicated
of countless years stuck in a vice?
What is rehabilitation?
A determined mindset on contemplation?
An addict must crave his cure.

MOTHER LIBERTY

You stand proud.
Standing for the ever pursuit of happiness.
A hope for the fulfillment of life and prosperity.
You stand with a burning flame.
Meant to illuminate the strayed at sea,
but you also stand on grounds that refuse to relinquish hate.
Bound to a society that promotes the evolution of a social caste.
Where one can be subject to an immoral compass
based on their outer appearance.
Even down to a simple draw of faith.
How can you stand with that heartless of a man?
One that wages war on that bias of liberty.
How can you be the product of displacement?
All the while you create the need of immigration.
Seen to many as a hope.
False truth flatters propaganda.
Seen to plenty as a hoax.
Often while freedom thinks of you.
My sweet lady liberty,
if freedom is dead
then so is chivalry.

BOUND TO

Remember the nights we sat up worlds apart.
You hummed the beat, while I spoke lyrics from the heart.
Creating a flow that seeped through the ripples of time.
You became my lover, a goddess in her prime.

A slave to the words of this endless rhyme.
We became two parts of a whole.
A family to a homeless love.
I became your diary.
A reality to your imagination.
Lost in rotation, an unbecoming situation.

Lost in thoughts of being together
we became lovers unbound to time.
In our hearts, we stood still
all the while the world around us
gravitated towards our will.

Remembering the nights where they were worlds apart.
When he spoke the words to the beat of her heart.
Bound to an endless de ja vu.
Devoid of what is understood.
I will always gravitate to you.
We are bound to be misunderstood.

She will conquer his ambitions.
Side by side through the test of time.
He will conquer her ambitions.
Side by side through this endless rhyme.

The seasons will come and go.
As will the memories of their past.
Driven by her lust for fate you'll see.
Experiencing the ripples of time.
Her soul will wait patiently at the edge of the sea.

All their moments of clarity would have come in solidarity.
Up until they lay beside each other at last.
He will enter her temple without a knock or a ring.
Silence bound to their tongues.
She will become his essence, manifesting
themselves as one living being.

ETHANOL DIGEST

Chivalry has no motive, but aims to please.
Time has no length, but is measured by its duration.
I wanted to be alone.
Weary from being used by those who had no intent.
Or the desire to utilize the thus of me.
I have lived but for so long,
but I have seen more than those who have come before me.

I write this to myself as a release from society.
Yes, I am imperfect.
My addictions have often rendered me homeless,
broke and without purpose.
I do not doubt my own shortcomings as a functional adult.
Who says that tomorrow I cannot awake to a dream deferred?
What forces stand in my way that cannot be overcome
with stamina and grace?
I will take all my desires and go forth with fruition and determination.

Hope is not a strategy, but it is merely a foundation,
a merit for progress.
An individual that can internally accept his wrongs and
forgive himself will overcome the opinions of others.
If those who care for you are too timid to believe in you,
do hesitate to believe in them.
I wish the best for everyone that I have ever encountered
up to this point.
I can no longer play a role that undermines my ability
to be at my full potential.
I will seek out retribution from this moment forward
in every action I take.
I hope that in my sorrow I will find harmony.

Larry Foster

Let those who have stood by me hear my plea.
I am here for you, but let me be.
Let those who I have brought shame and hate hear my conviction.
Today I place a barrier between the man that is known
and the man that is me.
I am secluded in my own thoughts and bound by no objective ability
to judge that in which I have not lived.
It is on this day that I address my health and current mental apparatus.
It is on this hour that I say no more and that the cure that
I seek is found within me.

Life, I ask in all your glory and fault that you bless me
with the wisdom to shine.
This is my truth.
As a young adult male, human and sexual by design.
I have lived a life of anarchy and desire for darkness.
I have tainted my flesh with the markings of peace.
Earth's drugs found its way into my soul.
But, I am not lost. Nor have I found myself.
I am at peace knowing that I accept this and that in due time, if I grow
myself and nurture myself, I will —as my uncle will say:
"Climb to new heights!"

Forgive my sins, but know my wrath.
I take a step forward towards independence and a step
away from dependency.

CONFESSIONS OF A LIAR

The title seems appropriate.
But if you believe a word I wrote
then you probably only read the cover
and not the context.

What is he talking about?
If you never listen
then you'll never learn.
But how do you know what's real
if you've never been taught?

The only way to know a lie
is to trust the one who is speaking.
Love has a funny way
of blinding the weak.
Time has a funny way
of showing us our weakness.

Funny thing is I never lie,
but people hear with their perception.
And everyone knows you hear what you want,
because they can't handle the truth.
They want to see you how they want to see you.
Love has a funny way of blinding the weak.

Is a lie even a lie,
if it teaches you a lesson
about trust, about life?
If you never trust anyone
then you'll never be lied to.
Confessions will only become their truth.

ABOUT THE AUTHOR

Larry Foster is a Johnson and Wales graduate, freelance hotel consultant, poet, and travel enthusiast from Atlanta, GA. Traveling the world at an early age led him to dedicate the beginning of his career to the hospitality industry and evolve an appreciation for unconventional architectural designs. Larry's life experiences were the pathway for him to influence the world by turning pain and affliction to glorifying awakening through his writing. Larry's essential goal for his readers is to dig deep into their heart to discover their motives and reasoning of life within their own perspective.

In the words of Larry, "A passion can only be understood by those who created art because they were misunderstood."

CPSIA information can be obtained
at www.ICGtesting.com
Printed in the USA
FFOW03n1223010518
46428947-48284FF